I0482941

Outsourcing Essentials

How To Start Outsourcing
for Freelancers
and Contractors.

By Matthew Harding

About The Author.

Introduction.
Who is this book for.

Chapter 1.
What is Outsourcing?
Terminology, Words, terms and definitions.

Chapter 2.
Why become an Outsourcing Freelance Contractor ?

Chapter 3.
What are you good at ?
Assessing your skills.
How much to charge.

Chapter 4.
Where can you find work ?
Outsourcing websites.

Chapter 5.
Outsourcing bonus video.

Chapter 6.
How to apply for a contract, and actually get the job.
What to do, what to ask, what to say.
How NOT to apply.

About The Author:

Matthew Harding is based in Melbourne, Australia. He is a husband, a father, a musician, a computer nerd, a lover beer and of the internet. He has several internet related small businesses and websites. He has many and varied interests, ranging from music to website creation, and is constantly amazed by the power of the internet.

Like all small business owners, he has tried to "do it all". Then he discovered he simply did not have the time nor the expertise required to do everything....

So Matthew did some research and finally dipped his toe into the outsourcing waters.

The benefits of outsourcing quickly became apparent. His productivity soared, as did his website rankings and traffic, and ultimately his sales. He has had many successes regarding his outsourcing experiences. But he has also made several mistakes and had several failures as well.

This book is Matthews' attempt at explaining his outsourcing experiences, in the hope that others will save time, save money and ultimately learn and benefit from these experiences.

He has been able to provide the necessary tools to hundreds of customers in order to help them with creating their own DIY Websites – http://www.DIYWebsitesByMatt.com .

He has composed, recorded and sold thousands of relaxation music CDs and digital downloadable albums – http://www.RelaxationSuccess.com , http://www.RelaxationMusicAustralia.com and http://www.SimplyRelaxation.com

If you wish to start your own business reselling domain names, website creation tools, hosting and many other website services, Matthew has made these available via http://www.ResellerByMatt.com

 Follow me on Twitter -
https://twitter.com/MatthewHarding
@MatthewHarding

http://www.HowToStartOutsourcing.com

Introduction.

Who is this book for ?

Are you stuck on a treadmill, running in the seemingly never ending cycle of "get up, go to work for someone else, come home, go to bed. Repeat." ?

Perhaps you think (perhaps you know!!) that you can do a better job working for yourself ?

Maybe you are thinking that there must be more to life than Working For The Man ?

Or, are you currently "unemployed", and looking for something – anything – that might provide both an income and a sense of relevance or usefulness ?

You know you have some or even many skills that are marketable, useful, sought after - skills that others will pay for. Perhaps you are even using these skills in your current job or within your hobbies. Are you dreaming of a career change, a change of direction ?

It might be the case that for many and various reasons you are unable to find your "dream job".... or any job. And therefore you need to create your own job.

Would you rather get paid to do something you love, or are good at doing ?

This Book Is For You.

If you can resonate with and mentally answered "YEAH !!", or "It's like he's reading my mind !", to any or all of the above questions, then this book will help you.

We will explore some ideas and concepts to help you work out what it is you are good at and what you can offer other individuals, Entrepreneurs, businesses small and large, near and far, in terms of offering to help them make their lives easier. And get paid for your help.

We will explore the Whats, the Whys, the Wheres and the Hows of getting started in your outsourcing career. Working for yourself, as a freelance contractor, is a business - don't forget to treat it as such.

In Chapter 8 - by far the longest chapter of this book - we will hear the experiences of real outsourcing contractors and freelancers.... there are some common themes that you can learn from, as well as some individual gold nugget suggestions. These freelancers are from all over the world - North America, Europe, Asia, Middle East, Africa - each with differing backgrounds and areas of expertise. You will read about the lawyer, the translator, the SEO and marketing expert, the musician, the web programmer, the writer, the student, the virtual assistant and more - and how they got started with outsourcing.

Maybe you are looking for a career change. Maybe you are looking to generate a bit more income to supplement your "day job" on the side. Maybe you are unemployed (accidentally or deliberately) and are looking for options. Maybe you would rather work for Yourself.

Outsourcing Essentials: How To Start Outsourcing for Freelancers and Contractors can help you !

Chapter 1.

What is Outsourcing?

Outsourcing can have many different meanings in this modern day and age.

However, let's try to keep it simple:
Outsourcing - getting or giving help, usually with a financial transaction involved.

Within a business situation, this can mean the hiring of staff for a permanent role, or it could mean hiring someone to perform a "once off" task, or perhaps a "regular" task once a week, once a month, etc.

Within a personal setting, Outsourcing can involve help with domestic duties like cooking, cleaning, picking up the milk from the shop or making an appointment at the dentist.

Sometimes, within a big business setting, outsourcing can be seen as a bad and horrible concept - making the entire IT and Customer Service departments redundant and sending the work overseas to another country, for example. While it can be arguably justified from a financial rationalisation perspective, this is perhaps more of an "Off Shoring" definition, and not what this book is about.

Outsourcing in the context of this book is about small groups of people allocating small or regular tasks to others outside of their immediate businesses. A "solo-preneur" or entrepreneur who is setting up their small business is too busy to do everything, so they need help.

A freelancer is someone who can provide this help.

Both the small business owner and the freelancer are seen to be Outsourcing.

Outsourcing means handing over business tasks or personal related tasks to other people, who are not from within the business. These people will take over a job or task that the business owner may not be very good at or may just have no time for. The Small business owner saves time and effort by outsourcing the tasks to other individuals.

Outsourcing is defined as a method of hiring an outside service provider to complete specific tasks for a business. It is similar to hiring an employee. However, in outsourcing, the business owner will only have to enlist the worker's services for the duration of the project instead of having to employ him for an extended or permanent period of time.

Additionally, the pay is often pegged per project instead of the number of hours the worker actually does work.

With the Internet, it's never been easier to outsource work to experienced freelancers. There are literally hundreds of websites featuring freelance portfolios and telecommuters looking for part or full time employment from their home offices.

In addition, there are dozens of online marketplaces where business owners can place a listing request for specific skills and locate hundreds of potential freelancers willing and able to complete the job. Similarly, outsourcing freelancers and contractors can display or advertise their areas of expertise, or apply for jobs posted by business owners

It's an invaluable asset that will help small businesses as a strong unit, one that is well managed, scalable, and flexible.

Outsourcing simply makes sense. Not only is it a great strategy of getting more done in less time, but it can be more cost effective than the business owner simply doing it all themselves.

Experienced freelancers can be essential to small business

owners and entrepreneurs.

Freelancers are paid either per project, or based on specific time frames, such as monthly, or on how many hours are dedicated to each project. A "project" could be as simple as a once off 30 minute task, or a two hour time frame, or a day, or a week, or a "please complete this by Friday" concept.

This means, that rather than being forced into hiring a freelancer on a full time basis, small business owners can work with them on an intermittent basis, giving them the flexibility they need.

Outsourcing is all about working smarter, not harder – for both the small business owner and the freelancer. A true win-win situation.

Terminology:
Words, terms, and definitions.

As with most industries, there is a certain amount of unique terminology – and the "outsourcing industry" is no exception. It helps to know the key terms and words in order to "speak the lingo" and have a vague understanding of what people are talking about.

Given the modern world we live in, most of these are fairly self explanatory… however, it doesn't hurt to go over them.

Outsourcing – the process of employing someone, or being employed, to do a task or series of tasks. This could be a "once off" task, or it could be "on going" for a specific time frame, or for years.

Employer – The business owner, the entrepreneur, the business, the company who is looking for a task to be completed. The Employer pays the Freelancer to complete a task.

Client – same as Employer.

Freelancer, Freelance worker - A person who makes their living by doing work on a very casual basis, often "once off" tasks for multiple and varied employers.

Contractor, Contract worker – same as Freelancer.

Telecommuting, to Telecommute - The process of virtually going into the office to work. Someone who "works from home" for their employer, using their computer and usually the internet, is said to be telecommuting to work. Virtual commuting, as opposed to physical commuting.

Post a job – to advertise a task or requirements, with the goal of finding a Freelancer. Usually done on an outsourcing website.

Profile – an "about me" page or paragraph on an outsourcing website, describing the skills and/or services available from a Freelancer or Business Owner. This is essential for Freelancers, and can be modified as skills evolve !!

Listing – see "Post a job".

Project – another term for a job or task.

Contract, or Agreement – a simple, written agreement between an Employer and a Freelancer. Often the details are agreed to during the course of discussions (usually via email) during the negotiation process. The various outsourcing websites usually provide default contract wording and conditions. The beauty of outsourcing simple tasks to Freelancers is that usually a contract or agreement really is very simple – "I will pay you $X if you do Y task for me".

Chapter 2.

Why become an Outsourcing Freelance Contractor ?

Freelancer contractors can pick and choose the jobs and tasks they wish to undertake. They can choose their rates of pay. They can choose when and where they complete the tasks – to fit in around their families, their leisure activities, their location.

People often think of outsourcing jobs as moving a call centre to India or moving manufacturing jobs overseas. But the term outsourcing can also simply mean using someone else's help to get a job accomplished and completed.

Here is a list of different things that can easily be outsourced simply by finding qualified people online.... Are you one of the people who can provide these services ?

- Writing – brochures, articles, manuals, instructions, website content, reports, even books, etc.
- Copywriting, editing, rewriting.
- Article submission
- Music Composition
- Video Creation and submission.
- Graphic design – logos, artwork, letterheads, business cards, website graphics.
- Web content
- Website programming and coding
- Web tool development
- SEO Content
- Chat room and forums moderators and monitors
- Live Help assistants
- Scheduled maintenance
- Virtual assistants/secretaries
- Bookings, schedules, appointments, calendar / diary updates.

- Telephone help or (online) Customer support for your customers.
- Publishing assistance
- Ebay listings
- Court document research
- Photography
- Keyword research
- Research in general- competitors, blogs in your niche, contact details.
- Backlinking for your website
- Admin help, book-keeping, virtual filing and sorting.
- Form submission
- Technical support, such as website creation or design, IT issues.
- Blog creation, blog commenting, blog content writing.
- Customer surveys
- Ordering, inventory or stock control, dealing with buyers or suppliers
- Etc

These are just a few examples of the many different jobs available online through various outsourcing resources. There are hundreds of thousands of qualified people who actually make their living freelancing on the web. With the help of outsourcing websites, you can connect with high quality people and businesses who need your help, your skills, your expertise and the essentials you have to help them succeed.

There are plenty of freelance jobs that are available on the Internet and you can definitely find highly specific roles/tasks/jobs in whatever kind of imaginable niche, from article writing to the virtual assistant. The marketplace for freelancing jobs let you register as a contractor and post your skills (known as your "profile"), sometimes for free or occasionally for a small fee. Once your profile has been posted, you can begin to apply for jobs and put in bids or offers for available projects.

Chapter 3.

What are you good at ?
Assessing your skills.
How much to charge.

So, you wish to investigate the possibility of becoming a freelancer. Excellent idea !!

This instantly raises a few questions. "How do I start ?". "What am I good at ?".

If you are reading this book, you probably have a fairly good idea about what you can do, or what you are good at, and therefore what service or skill you have to offer your prospective clients or employers.

However, perhaps you are not so sure... If this is the case then the first thing to do is to make a list of everything that you think you are good at.

Grab a pen and a piece of paper and write down the answers to these questions.

By actually going through this exercise and actually writing down the answers, you will begin to generate thoughts and ideas that will bring in turn create some "Aha !" moments. Who knows – maybe you have a fantastic business idea just waiting to reveal itself ?

Got your pen and paper ready ? Good.

Are you looking to leave your current job to begin freelancing ? What did you do in your "old" job ? Did you enjoy it ? Were you good at it ?

What do you enjoy doing ?

Do your friends and family ask you for help in one particular area over and over again ? What do other people ask you for help with ? For example, does your Father-In-Law telephone you almost every second day and ask for help with his computer, because he has broken / lost / can't remember / error messaged it again ? Do your friends constantly ask you to draw them pictures or design their logos ? Do you speak another language and therefore you are always being asked by your friends to translate this piece of text for them ?

What can you do quickly and easily – faster than anyone else you know ? Can you do clever things quickly with numbers and accounting ? Do you know your way around some particular software – music apps, illustration or graphics apps, video apps, programming or web creations tools ? Can you research and write stories or articles or product descriptions ? Can you sing, dance, play a musical instrument ? Can you organise things, co-ordinate people to achieve a common goal ? What comes easily to you ?

How do you identify yourself ? What do you think of yourself as ? When making small talk with people and they ask you what do you do, how do you answer them ? Complete this sentence: "I am _____ ." eg a musician, a web programmer, a husband, a mother, good with children, a writer, a talented illustrator, good a researching on the internet, etc.

How much do you charge for your expertise ? Ah…. The million dollar question ! Perhaps another way to look at it is, "how long is a piece of string ?" In other words, there is no right or wrong or definitive answer here. Obviously you want to charge as much as possible – per hour, per job, per contract. However, markets forces and competition dictate that charging ridiculously over the top rates will ensure you do not get too much work. Keep in mind that there are employers who are only motivated by price – they only want to pay the least amount possible. Also, keep in mind that there are employers who are more interested in quality and expertise and an excellent end result – and they are prepared to pay a premium for this. So, the answer to the "how much do I charge" question is….. as much as you want, at any given moment in time.

What do other contractors charge for offering similar services as you ? Check out the jobs currently being advertised. Are the employers offering $1 per hour, or $20 or $100 per hour ? If you are just starting out in your outsourcing freelancing career, I would strongly recommend that you do a few "cheap" jobs in order to get some good feedback. Good feedback means a good reputation, which in turn means the ability to charge more and get more. Your initial primary aim MUST be to get good feedback – and keep this reputation of being an excellent, reliable and trustworthy contractor. From there, you can increase your hourly rate to a level you wish to aspire to. For example, a quick search of "web designers" reveals hourly rates of between $2 per hour and $200 per hour, and more in some cases. Who do you think will probably (but not necessarily) do the better job ? Most likely the more expensive contractor !

As a suggestion, check out the market. What do other contractors in your area of expertise charge, and what do they deliver for their fee ? What are employers offering or expecting to pay ? Are these figures compatible with your expectations ?

Can you offer over and above what everyone else is offering – in terms of service, turnaround time, skill, communication, after sales service, support, extra incentives – and thus can more easily justify a higher asking price ? Hint: the answer to this last question is, "yes, you can".

Another concept to get clear in your mind is about how much work you actually want to do. Do you want to work 100 hours per week ? Some people do ! Do you want to work perhaps a more normal "full time" week of 40 hours or so, but spread across 7 days rather than 5 days ? Do you want to replace your current full time job that you hate with a passion and that you have to commute 2 hours each way to get to a building you don't want to work in ? Or perhaps you might just want a few jobs here and there, purely as a smaller or part time income stream ? Again, there is no right or wrong answer here.... it is all about you.

Chapter 4.
Where can you find work ?
Outsourcing websites.

Here is a small selection of perhaps the more well known outsourcing websites. They are all very similar to eBay in that there are listings (or projects), categories, significant dates, as well as a familiar on screen layout. All of these outsourcing websites require both the employer and the contractor to "join" or "create an account" or "sign up". All of these websites have clearly listed fees (usually in the range of 5% - 10% of the job price or hourly rate), which the employer is responsible for.

oDesk.com

This site is extremely thorough, and it allows all of its freelancers to take a wide variety of skills tests. These tests can vary from typing speed to grammar, web coding to office terminology fluency and comprehension. Each test that a user passes is then added to their score, so that business owners can see how well each person did on specific tests. This is a great way to gauge how well someone will be able to complete a task for you, and a good resource for finding high quality work.

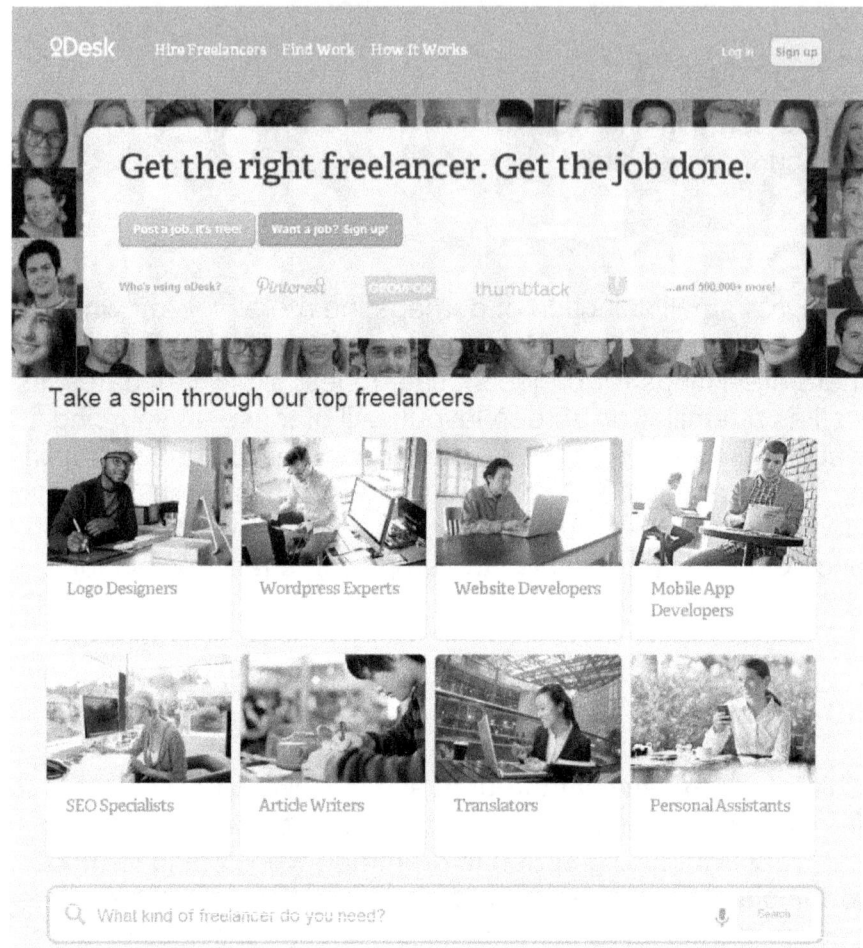

oDesk allows you to post your task in a kind of bulletin board style, where all users can see it by category, and then bid on the job.

The great thing about oDesk is that once you have hired a contractor and they have begun work for you, you can "see" how they are going and what they are doing. The contractor must log in to the oDesk website when working for their employers. The oDesk website system takes screenshots of the contractors computer screen every few minutes and the employer can view these screen shots. It is therefore very easy to tell if your contractor/freelancer is actually doing the work you have hired them to do, or if they are simply updating their own personal facebook page (or worse) !!

The payments system within oDesk is easy to navigate. It is simple to create a set $$$ amount for a completed task, or for an hourly rate. You can even limit the number of hours a contractor can charge you for per week, which makes budgeting much easier and when combined with the working screenshots mentioned above, limits the amount of "padding" a less than honest contractor can attempt to bill you for.

eLance.com

One of the web's most popular choices for outsourcing, this site has a plethora of different projects you can post or view. Everything from marketing to legal, freelance writing to web programming is covered.

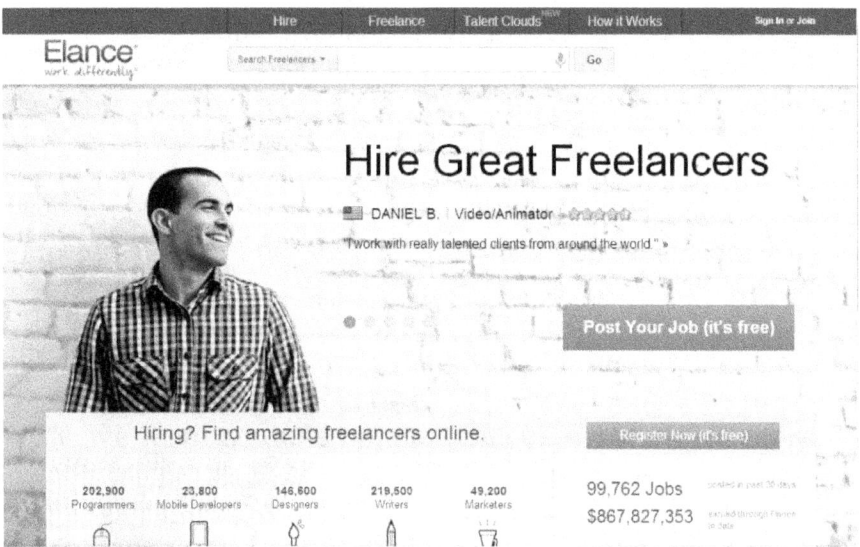

Get jobs done fast. Get the work done right.

1. Hire teams quickly.

Browse profiles, portfolios and reviews
to assemble your 24/7 online workforce.

2. Tackle jobs easily.

Collaborate in shared online work rooms
and receive daily activity reports

3. Pay freelancers safely.

Only pay for work you approve, plus Elance
takes care of all invoicing and taxes

Hiring a large team? Managing freelancers already? Learn about **Talent Clouds**

This is a one-stop shop for all of your outsourcing needs.

The site has helpful forums, video tutorials, and is registered with Verisign and the Better Business Bureau, so you know your investment is protected, and that you will receive quality work from elance members.

Freelancer.com   and   Freelancer.com.au

According to the Freelancer.com website :
" *Freelancer.com is the world's largest freelancing, outsourcing, and crowdsourcing marketplace for small business. With over 8 million users, you can hire a freelancer to do your contract work at a fraction of the cost. Whether you need PHP developers, web designers, or content writers, you can outsource jobs within minutes. Browse through hundreds of skills including copywriting, data entry, and graphic design or more technical areas like coding HTML, programming MySQL, and designing CSS. Are you an entrepreneur just starting a company? Find a quality graphic designer to create a logo to your specifications. Are you looking to grow your business online? Hire an internet marketer improve traffic from SEO and Facebook. Don't have a website or mobile app? Not a problem, we have thousands of web developers waiting to hear from you. Freelancer.com accelerates your businesses growth by giving you the talent you need when you need it. Once you get new customers rolling in, you can even hire customer support or a virtual personal assistant to simplify*

your life without the risky overhead and cost of hiring full-time staff. From beginning to end, Freelancer.com makes it easy to hire freelancers and find freelance jobs online. Join the thousands of businesses tapping into the world's largest marketplace of skilled freelancers. Post a project now!"

Hire Freelancers and Find Freelance Jobs Online

Fiverr.com

Fiverr.com gets its name from the fact that most jobs, or "gigs" as Fiverr.com calls them, are $5.

Again, as with the other websites mentioned, you can get articles or writing done, videos, music, graphic design, website help, IT help, personal assistance, and more. Fiverr also has a section devoted to physical objects such as gifts, as well as digital objects. They also have a sense of humour as shown in their "Fun and Bizarre" section where there are many weird, wonderful and wacky things that $5 will get for you.

Fiverr.com is interesting in that it is slightly different from the main "an employer posts a job and chooses an applicant based on the contractors who contacted them" model used with most of the other outsourcing websites. Fiverr's model is more of a "I can do this for you, do you want it ?" model. The contractors on Fiverr advertise their wares, so to speak, and if the employer wants what they are offering then you contact them to arrange the details… and it usually costs five dollars, or multiples thereof.

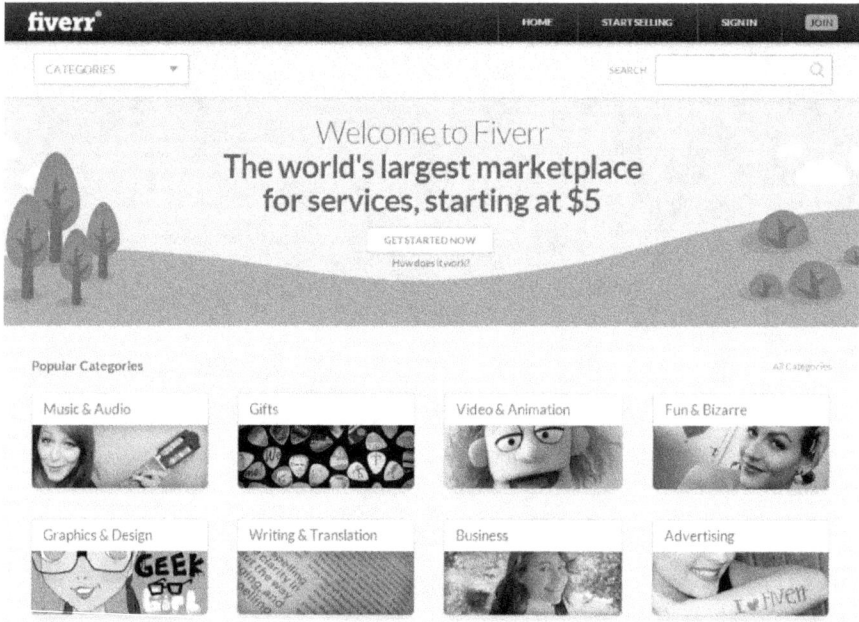

Again, there are search functions within the Fiverr.com website, so you can filter out what you do not want and find what you do want. There are some amazing things on offer…. If you want a video of someone dressed up in a hotdog costume reading a message of your choice, then for $5 it can be done quickly and easily ☺

For what it's worth, I used Fiverr.com to have the front cover of this ebook designed !

Setting up your own website is very important in this day and digital age. Without one (or two or even more), your customers will be unable to find you. It is really easy to set up your own website, and it can be done for less than $10 per month. If you can create a Microsoft Word document, or place an advertisement on eBay, or attach a photo into an email, then you are more than capable of creating a DIY Website . If you need some help with your website creation, then you can outsource this very easily. You will still need to buy a domain name, website hosting, website creation tools, but you hand over the details to your outsourcing contractor and it all just magically happens !! You might want to find another contractor to set up a Facebook page for you, or a blog, or a Twitter account, or a Pintrest page as well – but ultimately having a digital presence is possibly the most important business decision you ever make.

Chapter 5.

Outsourcing bonus video.

Outsourcing Tactics:
Video – Outsourcing Tactics.

Here is a fantastic video that I have made available for you. It gives a quick run down of several outsourcing websites, how to use them, what to look for and what to watch out for.

It runs for 18mins 30 seconds.

You can watch it here:
http://www.HowToStartOutsourcing.com/Video.html

I hope you enjoy it.

Chapter 6.

How to apply for a contract, and actually get the job.
What to do, what to ask, what to say.
How NOT to apply.

Applying (or "bidding") for jobs on outsourcing websites is a skill. Rarely is it the case where you just put your hand up to say "I'll do it !" and the employer or client throws buckets of cash at you.

A freelance contractor is running their own business – and applying for jobs needs to be treated as such. It is a business process, a skill that needs to be learn and perfected.

The first thing you need to do is spend some time setting up your public profile on each of the outsourcing websites you have signed up with. Have a look at other contractors profiles – what have they included ? What have they written ? What have they not written ? Would you employ them, based on their profiles, if you were looking to hire someone ? Learn from the good ones and the bad ones.

Another hint is to include a photo in your outsourcing website(s) online profile(s). The reason for this is to show that you are a human, with a nice smile. You are accountable, you are personable and you take your career seriously. Not having a photo conveys anonymity, and therefore causes distrust. Employers who distrust you simply won't hire you.

All outsourcing websites have a "featured contractors" section of some description. These are usually high performing and greatly in demand contractors who have completed multiple jobs, have excellent feedback and have been consistently working for quite a while. What do their profiles say ? Can you find one of these "featured contractors" who are offering similar services or skills to yours ? Obviously copying and pasting the text in their profiles is NOT going to help you at all – it may get you banned from the site, as well as irritate both employers and other contractors (not a good business idea) – but, can you use some of their ideas to describe your offerings ?

It is arguably exactly the same process as applying for a traditional job with a traditional employer. You need to be able to write a formal (or at least a semi formal) application letter. This needs to state who you are, what you are good at and why you are the best person for the role. As well as this, you need to be able to justify the amount of money you are charging.

Therefore, each job you apply for almost always needs to have a different application letter specifically tailored to the job you are applying for at that moment in time.

One trick employers use is, in the middle of their job description posting, they request you to mention their "secret word". This secret word will be something totally random and not related to anything as far as the job is concerned – it might be "unicorn", or "watermelon", or "rainbow", or "dancing frogs", or "singing elephants". The reason for this is so that the employer can see who is paying attention – who has an attention to detail, who has read and understood the requirements of the job being advertised. If you do not reply with the "secret word" then the employer will think if you haven't noticed this requirement in the applications process, what else might you miss if you get the job ? As a result, you will most likely be completely disregarded from the potential hiring – even though your price and your skills are more than perfect. Read the job description carefully !

Employers can tell very easily if you are simply recycling an application letter when applying for a job on an outsourcing website. Don't start your application with "Dear Sir / Madam", or "Dear Hiring Manager".... If they do not mention their real name, then use their online profile name, or use "Dear Hiring Manager at X company" as a last resort. Again, this proves you are paying attention to detail, and gives a very strong signal that you are interested in the job.

Do not apply for a job with a generic statement. Applications need to be specific and address each point or each request within the job posting. Generalising, being vague, being generic, and not addressing each point within the job posting are all great ways to ensure you do NOT get the job.

During your written application you will need to sell yourself. Explain your skills, your expertise, and your experience. Explain why you think your skills, experience, expertise are relevant to the role being advertised. Explain why you should get the job ! Explain how it will benefit the employer if you are in the role. Will you save them time, money, grief ? Will you resolve their issues and solve their problems ?

Here is an idea – to really blow away your competition and get you the job, why not actually do the job and prove you've done it in your application ? For example, an employer might have posted a job that involves the writing of a short 300 word article racing goldfish. Their job posting might have gone to some specific detail about what needs to be covered in this article about racing goldfish – maybe the best / fastest breed of goldfish, what food the goldfish likes before a big race, the best venues around the world. What is stopping you from actually writing the article ? What is stopping you from applying for the job with a simple sentence that says something along the lines of, "Dear Goldfish Racing Fan, the reason I am best suited to fulfilling your article writing needs is because I have already done it for you. Please find attached my completed article within this application. I hope it meets your requirements. Have a great day. Thank you."

What employer would not instantly say "**WOW** !", pay you for the article and leave you excellent feedback ?

And let's say that they don't.... maybe they might steal your article, use it anyway, and never get back to you with either comments or payment. Yes, this might happen. But it is highly unlikely. In this example, how long, really, would it have taken you to write 300 words when the brief in the job posting was clear and concise ? 15 minutes ? 30 minutes ? As long as it would have taken the other applicants – your competition – to write their application letters to the employer ? Exactly - not very long at all. And if the employer does "rip you off" in this example, it means they would probably have done so anyway, and the job would have been difficult, frustrating, time consuming and full of grief. By completing the task in this example, you have saved both yourself and the employer a lot of time.

Chapter 7.

Getting Paid.
Fees and Charges.

The main reason you are providing your services and skills to your Employers is most likely to be for the money. Yes, you are good at what you do, yes you enjoy and derive satisfaction from various and multiple concepts behind being an outsource contractor…… but ultimately your main catch cry is probably, "show me the money !"

The good news is that almost all official outsourcing websites (especially those shown is Chapter 4) handle this important part of the whole transaction for you.

Essentially, the process is similar to this:
1. The Employer registers a payment option with the Outsourcing website.
2. The Outsourcing website verifies this payment option.
3. The Employer can then proceed to advertise the requirements.
4. The Employer and the Contractor agree to terms (money, timelines, deliverables, payment and key milestones, etc) and enter into a simple contract.
5. The Contractor can and should expect to receive a deposit or up front payment consisting of a percentage of the entire job.
6. The Employer and the Contractor agree that key milestones have been reached, and funds are released to the Contractor, if applicable.
7. Employer and the Contractor agree that the job is complete and the remaining funds are released to the Contractor.
8. The Outsourcing website handles and controls these payments, and acts as umpires if disputes arise.

Effectively, the Employer pays the Outsourcing website, and the Outsourcing Website then pays the Contractor.

What this means is that you as the outsourcing Contractor are almost guaranteed to get paid !!

This works really well in 99.9% of cases, which means that everyone is happy 99.9% of the time – which is really great.

Occasionally there may be a dispute between the Employer and the Contractor – however, keep in mind this happens in physical employment situations as well as in virtual telecommuting situations. The good outsourcing websites have systems and policies and processes in place to resolve the few issues that do occur so that the end result is one where both parties have a satisfactory outcome.

Note – most good outsourcing websites have a feedback system similar to that of eBay. The Employer leaves feedback for the Contractor, and the Contractor also leaves feedback for the Employer at the end of each contract / job. As a contractor, your feedback is vital. The simple (and only) way to ensure you have excellent feedback is to provide an excellent service or outcome for your employer(s) for each and every job. If you have excellent feedback from past employers you will get more jobs more easily. If you see an employer who has some not so good feedback, perhaps you might wish to think twice before agreeing to work for them…. This will potentially save you a lot of time and grief.

The Outsourcing Website makes their money via various fees – usually paid by the Employer, or via some charges usually paid by the Contractor. Usually these fees or charges are deducted by the outsourcing website at the moment of payment – the Employer pays the outsourcing website, the website deducts their fees, then they pass the remainder on to the Contractor.

To follow is a summary of the payments processes from the Outsourcing websites listed in Chapter 4, and how much of the total transaction the Contractor gets to keep, or is charged.

ODesk.com

The following text has been copied from the oDesk website, and is correct at time of writing.

How does oDesk guarantee payment?
At oDesk, an hour worked is an hour paid. Our Work Diary system tracks your time and takes snapshots of work in progress, creating visibility into hours worked for both you and your client to avoid disputes and ensure timely payment.

How often will I get paid?
Hourly jobs are paid on a weekly basis. Fixed-price projects are paid according to a schedule agreed upon by you and your client.

How do I withdraw money I earn through oDesk?
We offer a variety of ways to withdraw money from your oDesk account. Depending on your country, these include ACH, local funds transfers, PayPal, Moneybookers, pre-paid debit cards, and wire transfers.

How do I increase my chances of getting hired on oDesk?
The single most important thing you can do to attract clients and land jobs is to build an effective, impressive, and accurate profile.
Include all your relevant skills, experience, education, and a professional looking picture. Bring your work to life with a portfolio and build credibility by taking oDesk tests. And once you're hired, do a great job for your client. This will lead to top-notch feedback and new work opportunities.

How much does oDesk charge?
It is always free to sign up, apply, post a job and interview for jobs. If you get a job and get paid, oDesk charges a fee

equivalent to 10% of the total amount charged to your client. For example, if your rate is $18 per hour, oDesk charges an extra $2 so that your client pays a total of $20 per hour.

The oDesk fees are perhaps the easiest to calculate and understand. It is simply a case of subtracting 10% from the amount the Employer agrees to pay. Eg: Employer pays $20 per hour. oDesk takes 10% = $2. Contractor gets $18 per hour. Easy.

Further information:
https://www.odesk.com/info/howitworks/contractor/

Freelancer.com

Freelancer.com Fees and Charges

Freelancer.com fees and charges are a little complicated. For both contractors and employers there are membership plans – starting at zero dollars per month for the "basic" plan, up to $49.95 per month for the "premium plan". Then there are percentage of total cost per job / per hour fees which range from 3% to 10% depending on your membership plan, and depending on whether you are the contractor or the employer. Freelancer also differentiates between "Projects" and "Hourly Rates" and "Contests", which also affect the fees / charges.

The different membership plans allow greater opportunities to apply for jobs, or to post jobs. The free and "Basic" plan is more than adequate for a new contractor or employer. However, if the contractor starts to employ their own staff, or the employer is posting many, many jobs then the other monthly plans might be worth investigating.

For freelancers on Freelancer.com, you need to become a

"member" and subscribe to a "membership plan".

The following text has been copied from the Freelancer website, and is correct at time of writing.

For Freelancers
Freelancer.com is free to sign up, create a profile, select skills of projects you are interested in, upload a portfolio, receive project notifications, discuss project details with the employer, bid on projects (free members receive initially 8 bids per month) and enter contests.

For fixed price projects, if you are awarded a project, and you accept, we charge you a small project fee relative to the value of the selected bid, as an introduction fee. If you are subsequently paid more than the original bid amount, we will also charge the project fee on any overage payments.
For hourly projects, the fee is levied on each payment as it is made by the employer to you.

Membership Plan	Freelancer Project Fee	
	Fixed Price Projects	Hourly Projects
Free	10% or $5.00 USD, whichever is greater	10%

Membership Plan	Freelancer Project Fee	
	Fixed Price Projects	Hourly Projects
Intro	10% or $5.00 USD, whichever is greater	10%
Basic	10% or $5.00 USD, whichever is greater	10%
Plus	10% or $5.00 USD, whichever is greater	10%
Standard	5% or $4.00 USD, whichever is greater	5%
Premium	3% or $3.00 USD, whichever is greater	3%

Membership Plans
Select from a range of membership plans to determine the fees you pay for our service. You can work on the site as either an employer or freelancer as a free member, or gain additional benefits as a paid member by upgrading to a paid plan.

Memberships will recur on a monthly basis on the anniversary of your subscription, unless cancelled. If funds are insufficient we will try to renew your membership for up to 30 days, until funds are made available.
You may cancel your membership at anytime from the membership upgrade page, which will cease billing at the end of your subscription period without additional costs.

Further information
http://www.freelancer.com/feesandcharges/

Fiverr.com

The following text has been copied from the Fiverr website, and is correct at time of writing.

Fiverr must be paid somehow. They receive 20% of every order you complete, so $1 per $5.

See more at:
http://forum.fiverr.com/discussion/13855/answers-to-common-questions#sthash.xr77jgrb.dpuf

A service offered on Fiverr® is called a Gig®.
Gigs® on Fiverr are offered for a fixed, base price of $5 (also referred to as one Fiverr®).
Whenever you see "I will _for $5", it means the seller is offering a Gig® for the fixed price of $5.
Only registered users may buy and sell on Fiverr. Registration is free.

Sellers
Basics
Each $5 Gig you sell and successfully deliver, accredits your account with a net revenue of $4.
Buyers pay Fiverr for orders in advance.

Fiverr accredits sellers once an order is completed.
Sellers may withdraw their revenues via paypal. Note that
Paypal charges fees for this, not Fiverr.

Further information
http://www.fiverr.com/terms_of_service

Elance.com

The following text has been copied from the Elance website, and is correct at time of writing.

Employers.
How much does Elance cost?
It's free to join, post jobs, and see your candidates on Elance. We add an 8.75% fee to your freelancer's bid. You see and pay this price only, when you approve work.

You can use your MasterCard, Visa, American Express, PayPal or an Elance Account to pay freelancers. Your financial information is safe and will not be shared.

Freelancers.
How much does Elance cost?
It's free to join Elance and submit job proposals to clients. We add an 8.75% service fee to the price you quote for a job. When your client pays you, we deduct the fee and pass the rest on to you.

You get paid through your Elance account. Client payments are deposited into your Elance account, allowing you to make withdrawals right away. You're in control of when and how often you get paid. For fixed price jobs, you and your client will agree on payment dates. For hourly jobs, you'll get paid each week when you use Elance's Tracker tool.

As a general overview, Elance is free to join and there are no charges to post jobs, submit job proposals or work on jobs. Elance deducts an 8.75% service fee to all invoices submitted by freelancers. To help freelancers understand the final payment amount they will receive on their invoices, the service fee will show to freelancers as they calculate their bid. So, a client will receive a bid of $547.95 ($500 + 8.75% fee of 47.95) if the freelancer is aiming to receive $500 for their work. When work is completed and approved by the client, Elance collects the $547.95 payment from the client and passes $500 on to the freelancer.

This is the only required cost of using Elance. There are optional costs for clients and freelancers looking to enhance their success on the platform, but they are voluntary fees. See Membership Plan options for freelancers.

http://help.elance.com/entries/24080518-What-are-the-freelancer-membership-plans-

There are several options for withdrawing funds:
If you are in the United States, you can withdraw by Automated Clearing House (ACH) bank transfer, check, the Elance Prepaid MasterCard or PayPal. More Info
If you are in Canada, you can withdraw via wire transfer, check, the Elance Prepaid MasterCard or PayPal. More Info
If you are outside the United States and Canada, you can withdraw by wire transfer, the Elance Prepaid MasterCard or PayPal.

Further information:
https://www.elance.com/q/how-it-works

Chapter 8.

Real Contractor Stories and Advice.
Tales from the Trenches.

The following stories are from real contractors, with different areas of expertise, from all over the world – USA, India, United Kingdom, Serbia, Canada, Israel, Kazakhstan and Argentina. This covers a massive geographical spectrum, as well as across many different cultures.

I asked them all four questions:

1. Why did you become a freelance contractor ? What made you decide that freelancing was for you ?

2. How did you start outsourcing ? How did you become a freelancer / contractor ? What steps did you take to get your first / second / third / and more freelancing jobs ?

3. What websites do you use to advertise your services? How do you promote and advertise your services ?

4. What do you like and enjoy the most about being a freelancer ?

Here are their answers.

==

Felicity H. - **United Kingdom**
Main freelance specialty - Highly Skilled Writer

1. Why did you become a freelance contractor ? What made you decide that freelancing was for you ?

I decided to be a freelance contract as I wanted the flexibility it would give me. I like being able to choose my own hours, and make my work fit around my life, rather than the other way round. Before I was freelancing I was doing a lot of jobs that I didn't hold much interest in, but I've found that with freelancing I can pick subjects that hugely appeal to me, and subjects that I love to write about. I also hugely enjoy being able to build up relationships with clients personally, and work time and time again for people I enjoy working with.

2. How did you start outsourcing ? How did you become a freelancer / contractor ? What steps did you take to get your first / second / third / and more freelancing jobs ?

I started to outsource initially just through word of mouth. I advertised myself to friends and family, and soon started using outsource websites. I tried a few different websites, until I finally settled on Odesk, which is now where the majority of my work comes from. For the first jobs I took on I gave extensive examples of my work so that people could see what I was capable of, and when I had started to build up a client base I started to use previous clients as references.
Once I'd started to work for a variety of clients, I then started to build up relationships with these clients, and making sure that I was always available to work for them. I built up a CV with a variety of jobs that showcased the kind of work I could do, so that I had something to send out to potential employers, and I'd often send a sample paragraph along with applications so that potential employers saw the kind of work that I was capable of in the field that they were looking for.

3. What websites do you use to advertise your services ? How do you promote and advertise your services ?

I mainly use Odesk to advertise my services. In my experience, I've found that websites like this, and especially Odesk, tend to drive a lot more business than having a website solely of my own. With Odesk I can browse for jobs in the fields that I can like, and I can pick the jobs that interest me, and the jobs that appeal to me. I love how easy Odesk makes it to narrow down searches to exactly what I'm looking for. I find that it's relatively easy to advertise myself on Odesk, as when applying for each job, I can tailor the application around the job I'm applying for.

4. What do you like and enjoy the most about being a freelancer ?

I love being a freelancer. I love really being able to get to know my clients, and I love that I can focus on the kind of jobs I want to be doing. I've found as though I've built up close relationships with clients that I wouldn't have done if I were working for a large organisation, and that I'm really being able to get to the heart of what employers want. I have been able to make my work life fit in around my home life, and I'm able to make a career for myself doing what I love.

==

Varsha A. - **India**
Main freelance specialty - Research Work and Data Entry.

1. Why did you become a freelance contractor ? What made you decide that freelancing was for you ?

When I started freelancing as a part-time job, it was just following the path of others. What attracted me most was **the ease with which freelancers work**, especially, if I could get everything done with the Internet and a computer. The most attractive part of becoming a freelancer was the flexibility in doing the job, not like the regular office where I had to compulsorily devote specific hours; I can work at the time that is convenient to me. Through freelancing I can showcase my skills in different areas which make the work more interesting. It opened up new career option for me by **sharpening my skills.** It's a win-win situation where I get to learn new things along with being paid.

2 How did you start outsourcing ? How did you become a freelancer / contractor ? What steps did you take to get your first / second / third / and more freelancing jobs ?

As usual I was doing internet surfing and I saw some side advertisements where it was written work from home and earn it reminded me of some of my friends who were already doing freelancing., I got attracted to it and opened it and tried to analyse how to do the work. There were jobs in many domains, just it was I had to read the completely understand the requirement of the client. I clicked on some of the jobs of my work area and interest and started applying for them. I made my cover letter very clear for the client to know my creativity and way of working. My purpose was to draft it in such manner so that he might find me the most suitable for the job. I got my first freelancing job from a German client that motivated me to work and understand German language.

3 What websites do you use to advertise your services? How do you promote and advertise your services ?

I normally register myself on various websites and bid for jobs that are relevant to my domain. I regularly use oDesk, elance.com, freelancer.com, peoplehour.com and thefreelanceweb.com. The best way to promote my work is by making an attractive profile and writing about all the projects that I have successfully completed. Positive feedback from my clients also adds to my advertisement of work. Working as per the requirement of client and finishing the project on time creates goodwill and trust with clients. This way I even get referrals that benefits my work.

4 What do you like and enjoy the most about being a freelancer ?

Freelance work provides tremendous opportunity and alternative to typical office jobs. The most beneficial thing is working with my own flexible hours; I can dedicate my own hours and work at times most convenient to me. As a freelancer I can learn new skills, that includes combination of activities and broaden my knowledge in vast range of areas. I get the advantage to work with people of different countries which provide me International exposure and relieve me from being confined to one place. Working from home allows me to work with the clients of my choice. My income is direct result of my own efforts which motivates me to work harder.

Nely A - **Kazakhstan**
Main freelance specialty - Interior/ graphic designer, Russian translator.

1.
I am a student, doing my final year. A fear of job-hunting and not finding a full-time job after graduation is what motivates me now. And plus, some extra money is what all students need. "Student years are the best – enjoy being a student" it is what I hear more and more often from my parents, my friends who have graduated and now working from 9 to 6. It is what I don't want to do in my future, stay in the office for 10 hours on weekdays, and waste time in traffic jams, having only 2 days in a week to do what I want to do. That is why I decided to be a successful freelancer.

2.
 Around three years ago I've listened to an interview with a guy who started freelancing while doing degree, and day by day he became more experienced, left his university and stated travelling, working at the same time. Isn't it a dream of

all young people? That is what made me think about freelancing, but I used to be scared that my skills are not good enough to compete with other freelancers; I became more confident with time, after seeing some job posts on freelance web-sites which weren't actually complicated for my level.
My first job was unsuccessful; I got it around 2 years ago. I was trying first some popular Russian web-sites for freelancers. After a week or two I was assigned a job – making two very simple flyers which drag attention. But the client didn't pay; I got disappointed but kept applying to some graphic design jobs. I've read articles about rewriting, copywriting and realised that what I was doing in my high school – writing compositions in literature classes (actually we were just rewriting and expressing other authors' opinions in our own way); so I started applying to this kind of jobs; after a test short task got my first rewriting job, then another one...
Apart from that I had some offline freelance jobs which I was getting with my friends' help – making brochures, fliers, doing drawing assignments for juniors in our university. And so I've stopped online outsourcing, because didn't have enough free time, or just didn't take it seriously. Recently I've started it again, but more seriously and motivated.

3.
I am using free-lance.ru, which is popular mostly in Russia, Kazakhstan, Ukraine but it has so many scam posts nowadays :/. A while ago I've started looking on English-speaking web-sites such as freelancer.com and odesk.com. I prefer odesk, because it is free and gives more opportunities for newbies to show their skills.
Since I am just a beginner, I don't have much experience on advertising my services. I am doing a simple website now, where I want to place my portfolio and basic information which potential clients may need. Also, online portfolio will be more impressive and give better chances in job-hunting after graduation.

4.
Opportunity to try myself in different areas which are interesting for me: making illustrations for books, making technical CAD drawings, doing some logos, and there are always new job posts which suit your skills but you never came across before.

Another advantage I find in freelancing is opportunity to choose projects – I don't have to do something which is not interesting for me; and I don't' have to work for many years doing something which I don't like.

What I enjoy the most about being a freelancer is flexibility : it doesn't matter if I'm doing the job in the middle of the night, eating fruits at the same time, or travelling to another country, as long as I doing it right and finish in time.

Dan K. - **Canada**
Main freelance specialty - Lawyer, project manager, writer and teacher.

Why Did I Become a Freelancer?
I became a freelance contractor because I knew that I would be more motivated to work for myself, rather than for anyone else. As a paid employee for most of my career – I found it difficult to motivate myself because I believed that I could make more money and do more meaningful work as my own boss. This was a major risk; as a business lawyer and consultant, I was earning more than $100,000 Canadian dollars per year. Having developed non-job income streams, I convinced myself that in time, I could make more than that as an independent contractor while being my own boss. That's an irresistible combination.

How Did I Start Freelancing?

While in my previous job, as a consultant at the business and government relations firm, Strategycorp, I met some potential business partners – people that felt the way I did. Having used Odesk in the past as contractees, we discussed joining as contractors. It was a big change of mindset. Beyond Odesk, I knew there would be other opportunities to advertise my services. Knowing that I loved to teach and that my services would be in some demand as a lawyer, I've created profiles on a number of freelance tutoring websites. I advertise my services on all of these platforms using social media and by finding the right email lists for email marketing; for example, when exam time is on the horizon for university students, I advertise my teaching services by emailing students en masse, at local universities.

I have also proactively scanned the list of opportunities on odesk. It is incredible to see how many new work opportunities appear every hour. As a new contractor without a reputation on odesk, I am unlikely to receive too many job offers – so it is important to start by charging less than I ordinarily would and doing some tasks that are not specialized for my specific skills. Once I build a reputation on odesk, it will be easier to acquire higher-paying work.

How Do I Advertise My Services?

I use plenty of social media platforms to advertise my services. LinkedIn is my favourite. LinkedIn users self-select into interest groups. Some groups are more likely than others to have an interest in my services. LinkedIn allows advertisers, at a very reasonable price, to target specific groups. Facebook does the same, although it is generally a higher-cost platform. I have also advertised on facebook by building a page and encouraging people to "like" it.

What Do I Like And Enjoy Most About Freelancing?

The sense of freedom. The fact that I can choose what kind of work I want to do – and ignore the rest. As a paid employee, you must do whatever your employer tells you to do. I also have no need to get into an office. I can work from home. I live

*in a big city, but my commute is 30 seconds! I love that kind of
freedom, and it will be very difficult to give up if I ever become
an employee again.*

Rajveer T. - **India**
Main freelance specialty - Web Design and Development

Q1. Why did you become a freelance contractor? What made you decide that freelancing was for you?

Ans. *I have done my B.Tech(IT) and after that I have go for
interview to companies as web Developer and I got. But there
was not good salary offer to me. That company used to hire
project from odesk . And thus I think I can also hire projects
from my own id while working from home. And thus I choose
freelancing job.*

*As per my skills I have managing skills and I was very hard
working and punctuate. I have skills of software/web
development and designing. And I can hire projects my own
and handle them. That's why I think freelancing was for me.*

Q2. How did you start outsourcing? How did you become a freelancer / contractor? What steps did you take to get your first / second / third / and more freelancing jobs?

Ans. *I used to do every single thing myself. I've streamlined a
lot of the underlying tech behind impossible hired a couple of
team members, and started automating a bunch of processes
to make it easier to scale things as i start executing the plans
for growth around here. However, as started to scale, I
realized that I needed to start getting out of my own way. As
part of that, I've started to really focus on outsourcing tasks.
As I got my first job in a company that got project from odesk
and get a lot of money. And I started my work there and got a
lot of knowledge from that company. When I think I have entire*

knowledge to hire project my own and finish them, I choose my way as freelancer.

To get my first job I started to bid on the projects that was of lower rate e.g. $5 etc and I bid on those projects whose client wants to spend money to lowest rate freelancer. When I got project from this schedule, I move towards to hire project with little bit more like $50 etc and like it when I got good rating I move towards more high level and got plenty of projects.

Q3. What websites do you use to advertise your services? How do you promote and advertise your services?

Ans. *I used to advertise my services through E-zines. E-zines also provide excellent advertising value; the trick is to find the right e-zine for your target audience. Freelance writing sites also provide a great deal of information on all kinds of publications that might publish your efforts.*

I also use Facebook, Twitter, and YouTube. These are great ways to promote your business through social media. A good example of how this can be effective was illustrated to me recently when we had a power outage that affected some areas of our small community. One of the local restaurants posted on Facebook that they had power and were open for business and within an hour they were packed with customers. I start generating links of my website on the social media and also create pages of my business on social network and generate a lot of traffic towards my business.

Q4. What do you like and enjoy the most about being a freelancer?

Ans. *There are literally hundreds of reasons why you should become a freelance web designer, and three of the best reasons are financial freedom, creative freedom, and you can work just about anywhere you want to. As per my opinion the best one are we can work from anywhere, I usually work from my home that helps me to get in touch with my family members and home town friends. As a freelancer its easy money making, I got how much I work. And as per my strength I am very hard working and can work a lot of hours. And also* *it's very easy to find a bulk of clients from a single place .Thus I choose freelancer and I enjoy a lot while working here.*

Dejan H. - **Serbia**
Main freelance specialty - Professional health & fitness writer

My experience as a freelancer.

As I didn`t succeeded to finish my Faculty on time, I had to find a way to earn money. So I started working some masonry work, which was very hard. After few days, my body was exhausted. I had to find something less physically difficult. So I started searching the internet, to see how someone can earn money. I tried on different sites to fulfill some surveys, with no success. I knew there was a way to earn money via internet, but freelance sites were not familiar to me, as I live in Serbia. One day, while searching the internet, I read that some people work as freelancers. I knew my English is perfect and I love to write, so I decided to give it a try and created profiles on sites such as Elance and Freelancer, with no success. My profile was not so well organized, I didn`t take any of the tests and didn`t get any of the jobs. Now, I knew about freelancers, so I could Google it. In one article I read that oDesk is the best site for the beginners and I had to try it. This time I created a great profile, did a lot of tests, and I was ready to get my first job.

I knew that a cover letter was very important, so I decided to write it in a Word document and save it, so I can use it regularly. I remember applying to all of the jobs, with no success, but I didn`t gave up. One day I applied for some proofreading of a small article and I was hired. Finally, I was earning some money! Of course, that was a low paid job and I knew that money was not important at that time. It was very important to get a good review, which I did, so other employers would hire me. I made some changes to my cover letter, making it more professionally and also added some working experience and skills, so my profile was looking great.

Today, I work only on oDesk and I`m very happy. On a daily basis, I'm managing two Facebook pages and writing and publishing tennis articles for a client. Apart from that, I apply to several different jobs, like formatting an eBook for Amazon Kindle (I learned it using YouTube videos), writing health & fitness articles, etc… And to be honest, I usually get the job.

Working as a freelancer is great. You work when you want and as long as you want. You have no boss, so you are not stressed and most importantly, you can pick jobs that you like. You can take a day off, or even a week or a month. The only thing is that you will not earn money, if you are not work. The only thing you need to be careful about is getting paid. Make sure your client has a good reputation on the site, or ask for half of the amount in advance.

Inna I. - **Israel**
Main freelance specialty - Web Research, Seo & Marketing, Administrative

Why did you become a freelance contractor ? What made you decide that freelancing was for you?

After having tried several office jobs I had a clear understanding that a 9 a.m. – 5 p.m. time format was not for me. Neither did I like the idea of having a boss watching me work behind my shoulder. Also, I knew that getting up early is my weak point, and, with two kids, I could not imagine myself working only evening or night shifts. My strong side, on the other hand, is my self-discipline which – in my opinion – qualified me for becoming a multi-task self-employed individual. So, I can say that my freelance career started spontaneously but, in a way, it was also a conscious intent since all the other options seemed less attractive.

How did you start outsourcing? How did you become a freelancer / contractor? What steps did you take to get your first / second / third / and more freelancing jobs?

It was not easy to begin: to my understanding back then, a freelancer was a synonym of a super-knowledgeable guy who brands himself as an expert and charges premium prices for his exclusive services. I was a university student when I dived into the big freelancing pool. My first freelance job was through oDesk and the task was to help a company CEO with a sales proposal – it was a tough task then and took me about two liters of coffee and hours of research. Speaking from cost-effectiveness perspective the money was not worth it, but I was eager to deliver a great work and make the client happy.

Then I got hired again: this time, my client needed help with planning a brand new website concept from A to Z. That included website structure, sales funnel, navigation, convent and a site map.

I only take projects which I can truly enjoy, so I took this one – the idea of the website appealed to me and I jumped into market research, product comparison, niche branding and all the things that can make a website stand out of the crowd. This time I got paid some good money and the client seemed to be happy about my work.

My hardest work was not about learning marketing concepts and sitting nights writing website content. The hardest work was to convince myself that I can do it and overcome fear. The main steps towards independent work were learning, sending job requests, accepting job requests and learning *again from mistakes and successes as one.*

What websites do you use to advertise your services? How do you promote and advertise your services?

oDesk.com was the first website where I advertised myself in 2009 and started the freelancing career. First advertising website is like first love: since then I have been working primarily on oDesk.com and even now that it has merged with Elance.com, there has not been much difference to me. Another way of promoting my services is using writers' community websites where I post niche articles about marketing, working from home and anything that can help me get positioned in the right way. For the last year, for example, I have been publishing content on squidoo.com – one of my favorite publishing platforms.

What do you like and enjoy the most about being a freelancer?

I like the freedom of building my schedule and the wide choice of tasks. I am my own boss and this is the best part about freelancing. Another thing I like is the self-confidence it grants me and the sharp sense of reality – there is no one standing behind me, no one paying my social security and I do not get a stable pay check. Yes, it is risky but life is risky and sailing my own boat keeps me alert.

Sonya C. - **United Kingdom**
Main freelance specialty -
Accountant/Writer/Transcriptionist/Proofreader/Administrator

Freelancing

I am a qualified accountant and have spent the past 30 years working in different companies in various capacities. The last ten years of my career was spent managing an accounting practice. My family and I immigrated to another country, so this ended my career as I knew it. The country we now reside in appears to discriminate against older people. It is extremely difficult to find a post, even with all the years of practical experience I hold. The sheer frustration of job-searching is what led me to first decide on becoming a freelance contractor. I felt pretty confident about it because that is how I initially started the accounting practice.

It was quite difficult trying to find out where to start the search for jobs. My first port of call was to search for temporary jobs in the local area. This was mostly done by doing searches on Gumtree.com and on recruitment websites.

The next step was to search for online jobs. I did a Google search for work from home jobs and checked all the results carefully. The one problem I found with this method was that very few individuals and companies advertise for accounting staff on these sites. It is an extremely difficult niche to pursue, even if you have experience.

The first job offer in my field that I received was for data entry. I felt that I should take the job because it was a starting point *for bigger things. Much to my dismay, this did not happen and I moved on to writing articles and doing transcription. In this area of expertise, I found several jobs simply by applying for the ones that I was interested in. The advantage of doing different types of jobs was that it opened the world of freelancing a great deal. I have managed to obtain a short bookkeeping job, but that was not found online though. It was a part-time post advertised in the local newspaper.*

I use different websites to advertise my services. I mostly make use of Gumtree.com and Fiverr.com. I have now designed a flyer which I have been delivering to businesses in my local area. I have not had a positive response, but remain hopeful as it is a new venture. My intention is to set up a website where I can list all the services I offer. I am hoping that this will provide me with sufficient work. Besides this type of advertising, I usually search for work on sites such as Odesk, Elance and Guru.

The one thing I enjoy about being a freelancer is the freedom it offers. You can start your day at anytime and if you work with clients outside your time zone, you can quite easily manage your time effectively. Freelancing is slightly less stressful than holding down a high-powered position. However, this depends on the amount of funds you need to earn to cover costs and the number of jobs you have secured. If you are lucky enough to secure a range of jobs, with reliable employers, this type of work environment is ideal. You have time to do the things you enjoy doing. As long as you remain objective and manage your time effectively.

Jacob F. – **USA** (currently studying in Germany)
Main freelance specialty - Mathematics, Business, German

Freelancing is something that had appealed to me long before I actually started. I'm a college student, so money is usually tight and I had considered trying to do some freelancing to pick up extra income. I am a Mathematics major and I have experience teaching and tutoring, so I figured that would be useful somewhere. Between my mathematical abilities, my musical knowledge (I write and play music), and some other skills I've picked up through work and school, I figured I could probably freelance successfully. After electing to study abroad, I struggled with no success to find employment in my new country of residence and I decided it was time to give freelancing a shot. Furthermore, the ability to work from home and on my own time seemed much better than a set work schedule if I could pull it off.

At one point during my earlier college years, I was working on a start-up venture and learned about oDesk. Having never heard of it, I was amazed to see this incredible community of freelancers and employers, where you could offer up any sort of standard or obscure project and someone out there would have the skills and desire to tackle it. I joined oDesk as a freelancer, took a few of their qualifying tests, and started applying to positions. It was a bit rough finding work initially as some positions receive well over a hundred applicants so I narrowed my search and had some success. I found work that I knew I was capable of doing exceptionally well and offered to do the work for a price slightly less than what I would usually want, given the lack of credibility I have as a new freelancer. My first job went really well and I had fun doing it, and the work was beneficial in my own personal development as well as for the client. After landing a position, I got a better feel for how to craft an application and land gigs, and that gave me the confidence to continue to succeed.

As a new freelancer, I really haven't started to advertise my services outside of oDesk. I have become aware of the larger online freelancing community, and I plan on expanding my presence to other sites as well. As of now, my oDesk profile highlights my skills and experience. I do run a blog and manage a Twitter account, so perhaps I will utilize those to advertise my services as well.

I enjoy freelancing for a number of reasons. First, the ability to work on projects on my own time is a luxury I have not experienced in the past. I can negotiate a deadline with my employer, and plan when I will work and not feel tied down. If any events pop up in my social life, I never have to decline because of work. My favourite part of freelancing is the variety of work I get to do. I recently completed my first two gigs. One of them was creating a practice math exam for a middle school student, and the other was building a mathematical model of a social network within a city. The options are endless if you work hard enough to build a repertoire of skills, there is the opportunity to work on so many interesting things.

Chapter 9.

Common Themes.

Based on the stories from real Contractors in the previous chapter, you may have noticed some common themes emerging.

"Flexibility" is bar far the most common theme. Most Freelancers or Contractors are extremely motivated by the fact that they can work anywhere at any time for as much or as little as they like. Some are morning people – they like to get up and get working, then go to the gym in the afternoon. Some are night owls in that they like to sleep in, have a lazy lunch, then get stuck into their work late in the afternoon and work into the evening. Some Contractors like to fit their work in around their personal or social lives – the Freelancing mother takes her children to school then comes home again to work for her Employers before going back to get her children again in the afternoon. The ex-corporate business man now enjoys his freelancing flexibility by taking his laptop to the local café where he has a leisurely coffee while spending an hour or two working. The university student can fit his or her working hours around their studying hours. Some people take their laptops to the beach on hot days, some have a dedicated home office, some take their iPads to the mountains and ski for a few hours before coming back to the café for a hot chocolate and another few hours work. Travellers can work while travelling..... some travellers fund their lifestyle entirely by providing outsourcing services to their Employers and never actually stop travelling: they spend as much or as little time as they like in any one place before moving on. This version of the common theme of "flexibility" certainly sounds very appealing indeed !!

A variation on the "flexibility" theme is that Contractors can pick and choose the work they do. Don't feel like working much today ? Sure, no problem. Maybe you want to take the week off – go for it. Rather take on three simple tasks instead of one really difficult or challenging task this week ? Easily done. There are thousands, if not tens of thousands of jobs or tasks on offer at any one time on many, many outsourcing websites and private notices. You – the outsourcing freelance contractor – have the luxury of being able to pick and choose which ones you wish to undertake. You can expand or refine your search criteria on these numerous outsourcing websites to bring up exactly what you are looking for. Perhaps you might like to only design websites about Poodle Dogs for clients in New York. Maybe you wish to provide Virtual Assistant services to clients / employers based only in Melbourne. Maybe you draw really good cartoon pictures of cats riding bicycles – but cannot draw anything else – so you keep your eye out for only employers who need original illustrations of cats riding bicycles.

Another common theme is the idea behind being able to charge whatever you wish. You may wish to meet the market, or undercut your competition, or maybe you wish to set your price much higher based on the excellent results you will achieve for your employers. Starting on the lower side of the price points for your services, skills or expertise and building up and charging more over time is a common strategy. This allows for the gradual collection of experience, along with relevant and great feedback, which in turn allows potential employers that you are as good, or even better than other potential contractors….. which again in turn allows you to charge a little more each time. Fairly soon, it is not unreasonable to be asking for more $$$ than you might initially feel comfortable with, and actually getting it !

Another variation on this theme is the advice to start small, with the view of getting good feedback. Concentrating on the feedback first by taking on small, simple and most likely very cheap jobs will enable you to build up a reputation as being trustworthy, competent and reliable. Slowly this will allow you to charge more little by little and take on more and more challenging and bigger jobs. Like all businesses, big or small, when starting out there is perhaps a short term pain for a longer term gain. You are in effect running your own business, so don't forget to treat it as such. A "loss leader" small / easy job allows you to get your foot in the door. Once your reputation has been established you can begin to change what you wish – your $$$ per hour or your $$$ per project, the actual jobs you take on, the size or complexity of the jobs, etc.

Some of these freelance contractors mentioned the problem of not being able to find a "traditional" job. Be it their age, local economic conditions, lack of sufficient skills, unwilling or unable to travel to the "big city", all of these contractors appear to enjoy the fact that they do not need to leave their house to find meaningful employment. One person (whose text did not make it into this book) mentioned he was a fisherman on a small island off the coast of the Philippines. With the large cyclones and storms recently in his area, his boat had been destroyed, as had the local fishing industry. His mother was injured during one cyclone and she needed him to be close to her – not out on a boat for days at a time. There were definitely no other employment opportunities on his small island. So, suddenly his life was turned upside down. While his boat was destroyed, his internet connection was not. He has found new ways to generate an income via several outsourcing websites. Not being able to find a "traditional" job for whatever reason has been a motivating factor in many freelancers lives.

Chapter 10.
Next Steps.

Going through the exercises in Chapter 3 is by far the most important step. Being fairly clear (not necessarily totally clear) about who you are, what you can do, what you can offer your clients and employers is crucial. This is not Rocket Surgery or Brain Science. You do need to have an understanding of how you can help other people, and how to use your skills effectively. By writing down the answers to the questions in Chapter 3, you are not only clarifying in your head what and where you can fit into the outsourcing market, but you are also therefore going to be able to explain this to others. Explaining this to others, such as potential employers or clients, in turn leads to paid employment.

Setting up an account within **ONE** of the outsourcing websites mentioned in this book – or the many others available on the internet – is step number two. It takes a little while to learn your way around these websites, so concentrate on just the one for the time being. Check out other contractors' profiles on your chosen outsourcing website. Note what you like and dislike and act accordingly. Pay particular attention to the profiles of the "featured" contractors, or those who have lots of experience. Don't forget to upload or mention some experience you have, some examples of your work, some links to where potential employers can find out more information about you and your skills.

Part 2B of this second step of setting up your profile involves doing some of the tests that many outsourcing websites suggest you take. **oDesk.com** in particular has several tests you can take – such as Writing, English skills, MS Office skills, programming skills (eg SQL, java, unix, html, visual basic, and many more), specific software skills (eg photoshop, autocad, quickbooks, logic audio, and many more). Completing appropriate tests gets noted on your profile and show cases your skill set. Which in turn can lead to more job offers – "they took the test and passed, so they must know what they are doing !" is what employers will think about you.

Step 3 is jumping in the deep end. Apply for some jobs ! Start small, don't immediately target the multimillion dollar 5 year projects (well... you can, but without feedback or history within the outsourcing website you may not get the gig...). Are there a couple of quick and easy tasks you can complete in order to gain some feedback ? Don't focus on the money, just yet. Focus on helping others and providing wonderful service and fabulous outcomes.

Gathering excellent feedback is priority number 4. By completing a few smaller jobs successfully you will open more and more doors for yourself. Gaining a reputation and having the history will show prospective employers that you are serious, professional, and good at what you do. This may mean some of the work you undertake initially may not be your dream jobs. However, each step you take and each task you undertake will lead you one step closer to your dream job(s).

Step 5 is to begin to apply for jobs that you really want to do – in terms of the actual tasks themselves and in terms of financial compensation. Keep in mind the old saying "you must be able to walk before you can run". Each job you tackle can be one small increment better than the last one. Maybe you can charge a dollar more per hour this time than you did last time. Maybe this next job looks a bit more challenging, a bit more fun, a bit more exciting, a slightly longer project, one step closer towards your goal.

Step 6 is to "rinse and repeat". Set up profiles on other outsourcing websites. If you can, link back to your original profile on your original outsourcing website (some sites do not allow this). Or at least mention in words rather than links where you have been active, your feedback, your experience, as well as your skills and expertise.

Step 7 is to apply and get as many jobs on as many outsourcing websites as you want, all the while charging what you would like. Once you have the experience, skills and feedback, you can apply for jobs that you may not really want to do, but could do with your eyes closed, and charge a large amount of money.... You will be surprised how often your offer is accepted ! Remember, your ideal

Conclusion.

It is easy to become a freelancer or a contractor. There is such a huge market, all wanting a huge range of services and skills. This market is global – it is not unreasonable to expect to be working for employers in countries literally across the other side of the world. You can work for people who you will never meet. You can apply for jobs before you go to bed then wake up the next day and do the job while the client is in bed. You will be able to find something, a niche, that you can fit into easily. Be it programming, writing, data entry, virtual assisting, making videos, graphic design, writing songs, dancing in a panda suit – there is something you can do.

By embracing or refining your skills, or even just simply looking to see what is on offer, you can easily find work and help others with your expertise.

You can do it. Dip your toe into the outsourcing water. Using the ideas and concepts contained within this book you are now more than equipped to begin. You now know How To Start Outsourcing. If you have read this far, then why don't you make the commitment to yourself to Start Outsourcing – quickly reread Chapter 10 and go for it.

There are many "success stories" on these outsourcing websites – stories about people who started as single contractors working for themselves, who then needed help because they got too busy, who then in turn setup businesses and hiring their own outsourcing contractors to help them help their clients.

I wish you every success in your outsourcing endeavours !

==============================

Author Information.

 Follow me on Twitter -
https://twitter.com/MatthewHarding
@MatthewHarding

http://www.HowToStartOutsourcing.com

http://www.RelaxationSuccess.com

http://www.DIYWebsitesByMatt.com

Other books by Matthew Harding

Outsourcing Essentials: How To Start Outsourcing for Small Business Owners and Entrepreneurs.

http://www.amazon.com/Outsourcing-Essentials-Business-Owners-Entrepreneurs-ebook/dp/B00HO2KGN8

Website Creation: It's Easy To Create Your Own Website.

http://www.amazon.com/Website-Creation-Easy-Create-Your-ebook/dp/B00AKQICP4

Useful Resources

Handy Links:

HowToStartOutsourcing.com

http://www.HowToStartOutsourcing.com/Video.html

oDesk.com

eLance.com

Freelancer.com and/or Freelancer.com.au

Fiverr.com

http://www.RelaxationSuccess.com

http://www.RelaxationMusicAustralia.com

http://www.SimplyRelaxation.com

==

Please write a review and share your thoughts ☺